Short Stories I Hope You Will Enjoy

Amusing • Tragic • Educational

Peter Joseph Hickson

Ordering Information:

Prime Seven Media
518 Landmann St.
Tomah City, WI 54660

Printed in the United States of America

TABLE OF
CONTENTS

WOMEN
VIOLENCE

During the 1960s I was an ambulance officer nearly always one man to a car. This was a stressful time for me being young inexperienced and sometimes naive. I attended many calls with varying situations motor vehicle accidents, assaults, illness falls etc. Somehow, I managed probably due to previous training.

At the time I had not been involved in fighting or violence. The law at the time was way behind the times e.g. a wife could not charge her husband with assault by law. Being young and reasonably fit males would think twice about taking me on. Why the reader might ask? well i admit that I dispensed justice on some occasions during those years. Probably on about 8-10 occasions. I recall being called to a house where the wife was assaulted (occasionally severely). Often the man was affected by drugs and/or alchol and the screaming of women and children can be very upsetting.

Being an ambulance officer naturally I had no weapons. Suffice to say I used my fists to dispense some justice. On two occasions I recall being called to the same house where the same wife / partner was assaulted by her husband/partner.

Thankfully things have changed whereupon men can be charged with crime, removed from the household and women are a little bit safer. These days I am much older and I am thankful that I don't have to be a part of any violence.

DRIVING / ALCHOL

B ack in the 1960s the driving under the influence laws were inadequate. In those days I used to ride a motor bike. The Police were constantly pulling over motorbikes unfairly. to keep up quotas etc. Ther was no points system, breathalyzer or blood tests and liquor laws were totally inadequate. Late one evening after a time in the local tavern the writer was pulled over by the Police. At the Police station the officers said I was under the influence of alcohol which I denied. Luckly a friend was following me and saw what was happening and followed me to the Police station.

Part of the driving under the influence test was "to walk the line".

Each Police station had a white line painted on the floor. When asked to by the officer you had to walk the line. Observation was supposed to notice wobbling, slipping unsteadiness etc.

Now being young and fit one could perform the task with determination even after consuming alcohol. Luckily my friend was in the Police station at the time. His observation and later the Police officer confirmed that the task was completed without fault. My motorbike was left in the Police yard and I walked home.

ASSULT MURDER

T his story meddled with my emotions for some weeks afterwards.

I was working as a registered nurse in the jail system in in New South Wales Australia. The cell block consisted of three floors with 80 men on each floor. The jail was for remand prisoners only i.e. prisoners charged with a crime and refused bail. Their length of stay could go on up to one year.

One could imagine that prisoners got to know one another and their charges. Additionally, being head of a family was very common.

A new arrival talked freely without any sense of self perseveration or common sense at all. Rules of the remand center were that shoes boots were forbidden. The only footwear allowed were runners, sandshoes Nike adidas etc. The stupid individual let it be known that he was charged with rape of an underage girl.

The inmates got together to formulate a plan. Starting with staging a fight at one end of a wing which resulted in nearly all the prison officers to the area. The second part of the plan was then carried out, the individual was kicked to death by soft shoed footwear by others, care was taken not to use fists.

Eventually I was called to see if I could be of assistance.

The Police were called who conducted an extensive investigation, eventually the inmates responsible were charged and convicted.

LOCAL CULTURE STORY

This is a story about the Leichhardt area a suburb of Sydney Australia where around one third of the population is Italian speaking. After World War two many immigrants settled in the area. The mafia has a presence in the local area in a protective sense as long as one did not interfere in their activities (gambling rent control etc.)

A public housing home was vacated after the longtime residents moved into a nursing home. An indigenous family including a 12–14-year-old boy moved into the home. The family were not used to anyone telling them what to do. The suburb has many "mamas" (Italian widows) walking around the area on their own. The indigenous boy stole a few handbags from the "mamas". The father of the boy received a visit from some mafia soldiers telling him to control his son. The advice was ignored handbag thefts continued. Late in the night the father received another visit from the mafia soldiers. The reader can guess what happened next. The father was hospitalized with injuries Police enquiries got nowhere as no one knew nothing! The family moved out of the home. This story was told amongst the local residents of the area which I was one.

LANGUAGE PROBLEMS

This story concerns a registered nurse I worked with in the early seventies. At the time there was complete repository for nurses between known countries. In these modern times criminal records are checked and an English test is required to become a registered nurse in Australia. The nurse concerned was born and raised in New Delhi India. She learnt the English language in primary and secondary schools. Her husband wanted to come to Australia. Consequently, she requested to transfer her nursing registration to New South Wales Australia. The latter was completed without problems. Being experienced in emergency unit nursing she applied and was given a position in a small hospital I was working in i.e. permanent night shift five shifts a week. The unit had three RNs per shift on night shift. After a few shifts she requested to be rostered the same shifts as the writer. Now one would assume all would be OK in the circumstances.

However, the reasons for the change quickly became apparent. Some other staff had other languages as their first language English was often their second language. The nurse concerned requester me to approach the director nursing to facilitate the dual rostering of myself and her which was approved. The nurse from India asked the writer passionately, "Peter I have problems understanding the English patients and sometimes the other staff are saying ". Part of the requirements of the job were to fill out the information card (no clerks on duty).

1/ One example of difficulty for example: a disheveled man when asked for his address he replied "where I put my hat". Naturally his entry should read NFA (no fixed address).

2/ Another example was in the patient saying his knee was "frozen", in fact his knee was locked following injury.

3/ Patient complaining of GUT ache when in fact the client had abdominal pain (no concept of the word GUT).

4/ Presenting patient saying he was pissed fell over and hurt his hammer and tack. Initial thinking pissed had something to do with urine and zero idea regarding hammer & tack (Australian slang for back).

5/ Client presented saying he had broken his Warwick Farm. The latter is Australian slang for arm.

These are just a few examples of the difficulty the nurse had trying to match the use of English taught in India to English language used in Australia.

When taught English in India the model was strict Oxford English traditional variety. After a few months she was quite thankful to the writer and she learned quickly and quickly adapted to Australian life and the hospital.

The events in question illustrate the many and different interpretations of language of all types in multiple settings especially "THE LAW". Naturally the legal profession gains its monies in this particular area frequently and often!!

WRONG CALCULATION

The time was 1966 in Australia the federal government decided to change the currency. Traditionally we had pounds shillings and pence i.e. 240 pence = 1 pound 20 shillings =1 pound. The change over ten shillings to one dollar=100cents, calculations for say shopkeepers and others were much easier.

At the time illegal punting on racehorses' greyhound dogs and trotters were illegal as were bookmakers. Australia has more racetracks trotting tracks and greyhound tracks than any country in the world wagering is second nature to the locals. Government totalizer shops were in their infancy. During these times a hotel outside the local psychiatric facility conducted an illegal starting price bookmaker (on course bookmakers were taxed and legal). Most bets were taken by phone or at the hotel on Fridays or Saturdays (electronic facilities did not exist). Cliental were around 200-300 every weekend .Settlement occurred on monday evenings at the hotel. The illegal starting price bookmaker gave the cash payment details to his elderly father for the payout.

Now one pound converted to two dollars, in practice the bookmakers' elderly father got the calculation wrong in reverse. As a consequence, winning punters were paid out DOUBLE WHAT THEY SHOULD HAVE BEEN!!

The bookmaker lost around 100 regulars as those paid double changed bookmakers. The person doing the Monday payouts was changed. During this period, I had the occasional bet with the starting price bookmaker who had to cope with considerable criticism and of course laughter.

UNFORTUNATE POKER PLAYER

F ollowing World War two Australia received many migrants from countries worldwide. In the suburb of Leichhardt in the city of Sydney many immigrants settled there from Italy. The name of "little Italy" quickly took hold. The writer lived in the area for over 30+ plus years. One had to speak a little Italian to exist there. Most of the cafes' restaurants businesses were Italian. Norton street was and still is the main street.

This story centers on the action(s) of the Italian mafia .Being local one soon became aware of their presence. They left the locals alone unless they interfered with their activities. Norton street is a very long street where regular illegal poker games took place on Friday and Saturday nights above the restaurants.

Enter a man who we will call Keith who lived with his elderly mother one street from Norton Street. The writer knew him having a beer with him in the local pub occasionally .He was a simple man who worked as a cleaner when he could. He used to mention his exploits as a poker player, apparently, he was a regular player in the Friday night game. Things must have unraveled after a time. Naturally some mafia soldiers were at the game and they hatched a plan. Over several months Keith had a lot of games and booked up a large debt. I remember him telling me he owed over $5,000 (quite some years ago). Advice was given to him by others to stop playing and pay off the debt. However, he continued to play off the slate (continuing to borrow). About six months previously his mother passed away leaving him the house. The timeline continues to blur, several months later Keith appeared in the local pub his leg covered in plaster using crutches.

Eventually I got the story from a friend of a mafia friend. The mafia soldiers who were part of the poker games carried out their plan i.e. A sales contract for the house he owned was drawn up by a corrupt solicitor and presented to him at game to settle the debt .Apparently he refused until they carried their task His leg was placed between two chairs held in position whereupon another player jumped on his leg from a height until it was broken. They then carried him out to the street after signing the contract. Fortunately, the mafia gave him a few thousand dollars after the house sale to ensure he kept quiet under the threat of death.

WRONG
COLOR ?!!

This is another jail story. The man concerned was in the remand section following drug is charges. Unfortunately, he was playing squash before incarceration without an eye guard.

A squash ball hit him hard in the eye, unfortunately he lost his eye.

In Sydney, Australia the state artificial eye bank had about 5000 prothesis in storage, all colors sizes worth several million dollars. One must understand that the eye and the eye socket are a very sensitive area, timing is critical after injury. The eye circumference is critical when using a protheses .Arrangements were made to transport to the eye hospital for fitting. The federal government decided to cut the number of eyes from 5000 + to a much lower number to save money. The man returned to jail I kid you not with one brown eye and one blue eye, he became the joke of the jail. Some weeks later the correct protheses size and color were obtained from the USA.

HAPPY ENDING, unhelpful information was given that the prothesis supplied was the only one in stock the correct size to fit the eye socket.

CULTURE SHOCK WOMENS RIGHTS

Some years ago, I was working in a hospital emergency department. A young Indian woman seventeen years old presented for assessment accompanied by a group of men (some middle aged). At the start it was somewhat that comprehension of the English language was lacking. With the help of another Indian staff member (catering staff worker) the issues became clearer. The client and male relatives had recently arrived in Australia. The issues emerged

1/ The client was pregnant

2/ The accompanying men demanded to know who was the father when the conception occurred and where?

3/ The clients' rights tended to take an extremely distant need.

4/ The men (including her father) demanded answers now.

5/ Two men demanded an immediate termination (one individual stated she was promised to him by the parents).

6/ The concept that the young woman had ALL the rights in the first instance without parental or other influence angered the men attending.

Things became heated with lots of screaming yelling in an Indian language, the assisting catering staff member became quite frightened of the men.

There were no immediate medical problems. A professional interpreter and social worker were called to sort out the situation. Once the issues were sorted things became even more heated with increased yelling / screaming /threats. The Police were called who removed ALL the men from the hospital. The young woman was taken to a women's refuse by the social worker who instigated other support services (unemployment payments etc.) Follow up outcomes are unknown. This story highlights some difficulties and stressors placed on nursing staff in emergency departments.

TERRIFING STRESSFULL AND YES DELIGTFULL EXPERIENCE

This story concerns my first devastating experience. Being a young ambulance officer with limited training in midwifery. I left my ambulance station in southern Sydney to a maternity call in the southern suburbs. The nearest hospital was about 15-18 miles away, I thought the case was a routine transport. When I arrived (one man to a car) at the address I was greeted by a very anxious man. We went inside and the heavily pregnant woman was already in labor. Quickly I realized I would have to deliver a baby (my first). My training would have to suffice as lives depended on me, I had to remain cool and professional. In those days scans were in limited use, mostly multiple births were not known by the pregnant woman. Well contractions were close together

I realize birth was imminent I asked the husband to get the maternity kit out of the ambulance. The baby started to appear without problems and was delivered. Thanks to the creator that allowed my anxiousness to dissipate. I clamped and cut my FIRST umbilical cord. To my horror contractions continued and another head appeared in the woman's body. Luck and zero complications occurred thanks again to the divine creator. Both babies breathed spontaneously ounce again to the latter (one of each). At this stage I still kept panic, overwhelming feelings at bay. The parents had no idea they were having twins.

Some weeks later the father went to the ambulance station looking for me and delivered a case of beer. This day was one of the most stressful days in my life.

BETTING DAY
AT THE PUB

This a story about horse racing and betting. I was in a pub with friends on Saturday to drink bet and listen to the races in 1980. The best race of the day was the Sydney cup over 3200 meters (two miles) just after 3pm. An illegal bookmaker was in the pub taking bets. I placed a bet called a trifactor picking the first three placings in order. The bet was successful paying just over $1000. in addition, I had a bet on the third horse each way I.E. to win and place2nd and 3rd. The price was 400 to 1 so third place paid 100 to 1 the result was another $2000 WOW. The police raided the hotel and arrested the bookmaker. Naturally I and others became concerned about being paid. The time was now around 4pm. The punters were assured by the pub publican would return after being bailed. Around 6.30 pm the bookmaker returned and paid all the punters. By this time after celebration about half the day one was under the influence of alcohol blurring speech etc.

I became very anxious about how my wife would react when I got home. A friend of mine said give me $400 which I did he put a rubber band around the banknotes then put the notes in my top pocket. Next, he called a taxi and told me to go in the front door give her the WAD and tell her to shut up, then go straight to bed straight away. To my surprise the tactic was very successful.

For the record the placings were 1st Kingston Town 2nd Surround 3rd Marlborough

METHADONE PRIVATE CLINIC

T his story has many connotations to think about, sometimes I didn't know how to think, worry interpret or ascertain about my empathy frustration feelings.

NOW to understand heroin addiction and the use of the controlled drug Methadone. Herion use quickly becomes addictive (highly so) several times more so than one realizes. Users will usually do anything to keep up supply I.E. steal rob use up relatives' assault or any other means. Withdrawal is very severe the client becomes very anxious and desperate +. Mental processes become confused deranged misjudged often ill-timed wrong and illegal. In general terms addiction spreads across all levels of society educated and non-educated, the reader should appreciate this phenomenon. The reader concerns the use of Methadone. The Germans invented synthetic morphine in WW2 due to the lack of supply of morphine. In the early 1960s an American psychiatrist thought the use of the drug could help heroin addicts, trials were successful.

Research has proven methadone is very addictive however the benefits are the extreme craving is REMOVED (the craving of giving up cigarettes multiplied by about 200 times is how the opiate addict feels when supply is cut). Consequently, the the person can get on with their life (if they come to terms with their addiction) thus get on with their life i.e. re-establishes family relationships, see their children siblings' parents, get ofF the police watch lists, work pay taxes.

I now ask the reader to rethink the start of this story regarding emotionally anxiety feelings and thought processes. I am a registered nurse in middle life ++ helping a friend who was a director of a private methadone clinic in central Sydney. During holidays he asked me to relieve for a period. The job required the daily dosing of previously prescribed (by a psychiatrist) of methadone. I agreed to help out my efforts reiterate my earlier comments.

RULES OF CLINIC

1/ Present in a normal mental state i.e. .not stoned wobbling around etc.

2/ Pay cash or card for your daily dose.

3/ Be courteous to all staff.

4/ Submit to regular urine sample requests under surveillance.

The single toilet had cameras installed which could be viewed from the dispensing area.

A young client came to the clinic with a baby in a pram. She showed her identification and requested her dose. I conferred her prescription and dispensed her dose. Then I requested a routine urine sample. The young woman looked anxious then proceeded to the bathroom. Now being an oversized middle-aged man, I was reluctant to view the young woman micturating (pee) into the specimen jar. My sight and head movements tended to close up out of dignity. To my astonishment the young woman went into a bag in the pram then pulled out a nappy (dipper). Then proceeded to squeeze the contents into the provided specimen container. CLEVER, INGENIOUS, I couldn't expose her knowing the baby would be affected.